W9-DCE-504

Overdrive

Eric Walters

orca soundings

ORCA BOOK PUBLISHERS

National Library of Canada Cataloguing in Publication Data
Walters, Eric, 1957-
Overdrive / Eric Walters.

(Orca soundings)
ISBN 1-55143-318-4

I. Title. II. Series.

PS8595.A598O94 2004   jC813'.54   C2004-900490-5

Summary: When Jake is involved in a street-racing accident, he struggles to do the right thing.

First published in the United States, 2004
Library of Congress Control Number: 2004100597

Orca Book Publishers gratefully acknowledges the support for its publishing programs provided by the following agencies: the Government of Canada through the Book Publishing Industry Development Program (BPIDP), the Canada Council for the Arts, and the British Columbia Arts Council.

Cover layout: Lynn O'Rourke
Cover photography: Getty Images

In Canada:
Orca Book Publishers
1030 North Park Street
Victoria, BC Canada
V8T 1C6

In the United States:
Orca Book Publishers
PO Box 468
Custer, WA   USA
98240-0468

Printed and bound in Canada
on New Leaf Eco, 100% post consumer waste paper

07 06 05 04 • 5 4 3 2 1

For my son, Nick, as he turns sixteen
and gets his license.
—E.W.

Other titles by Eric Walters,
published by Orca Book Publishers

War of the Eagles
Caged Eagles
Three on Three
Full Court Press
Hoop Crazy
Long Shot
Road Trip
Off Season
Underdog

Chapter One

"Well?" Mickey asked.

I pulled the driver's license out of my pocket and held it up for him to see.

"All right! Way to go, Jake. You got it!" he said. He gave me a highfive.

"Did you have any doubts?" I asked.

"I figured you could drive, but a test is a test, and neither of us ever does so well with those."

"This is one test I was ready for," I said.

"So now you have a driver's license. All you need is something to drive."

"Taken care of."

"It is?"

I nodded. "Come and have a look."

Mickey trailed after me out to the driveway.

"Your brother gave you his car?" Mickey asked in disbelief.

"Not gave. Lent."

"That is so cool."

"He said that I should have a car to drive the day I got my license, so he lent me his for tonight."

Mickey laughed. "You have the best big brother."

"He's okay."

"Okay? The only thing my brother, Andy, ever gives me is a hard time."

"I've seen you two together. It looks like you give more grief than you get."

"Haven't you ever heard that it's better to give than to receive?" Mickey smiled. "But I guess it's only fair you get to borrow it when you consider all the help you've given him with his car."

"It's not like he's forcing me. I love fooling around with cars. Besides, he's taught me a lot of things."

"You mean your brother knows more about cars than you do?" Mickey asked. I liked the way he said that. It was like he couldn't believe it was possible.

"He knows more, but he's two years older." I paused. "So, you want to go for a ride?"

"Yeah, of course…where to?"

"I was thinking that maybe we could go for a little cruise along the Lakeshore strip, or even go to the Burger Barn and pick up a burger and fries."

"I am so there," Mickey said. "We are going to see and be seen. Let me get changed." Mickey rushed up the driveway back toward his house.

"What's wrong with what you have on?"

"Shoes would be a good start, but the rest is only okay for hanging around in my basement. Let me get changed and do something with my hair."

"Hurry up!" I yelled after him. "We don't have all night!"

I wasn't joking. We didn't have all night. My brother was getting off work at the grocery store at nine-thirty, and I had to have the car home by ten so he could go out.

I climbed into the car—climbed in behind the *wheel* of the car. I turned the key in the ignition and the motor came to life. It made a gentle purring sound. I revved the engine slightly and the purring got louder and more powerful.

This wasn't just any car. This was *the* car.

I'd worked with Andy to redo the engine—torqued it so it put out over 300 horsepower. We'd redone the exhaust system to deal with the extra power. We'd overhauled the suspension to get the frame lower to the ground. It allowed it to be more stable at high speeds, especially around corners. My brother wanted this car to fly but not actually take flight.

He'd put on special lights—all customized front and back. Then he'd added a rear spoiler, and last week we'd tinted all the windows. It was cool to be able to look out but not have people see who was looking at them. Now we were doing the final work—redoing the body and putting on a new paint job. The body hadn't been bad—it had a few rust spots and a couple of little dents and scratches—but he was redoing it completely. We'd taken off all the emblems and letters that identified the make of the car. Andy said that Chevy may have made the car originally, but he'd made it better and he didn't want to share credit with them. There were patches of body filler and primer paint, and it had all been sanded down in preparation for the new paint—the red paint—that was being put on next week. Red did seem like the right color. Certainly a lot better than the sort of off brown, sort of dark gray, hard-to-describe color it was now.

Mickey ran down his front walk and along the driveway. His shirt was undone, he was carrying his shoes, and his pants were on so low it looked like he was in danger of tripping over them. When he said he wanted to get changed, I didn't think he meant in the car.

Mickey jumped in the passenger seat. "Let's roll!"

Chapter Two

"So is this just a one shot-thing, you borrowing your brother's car?" Mickey asked.

"Nope. He said that as long as I help and kick in some money for gas and repairs, I can use the car sometimes."

"Fantastic! And this just about makes it official," Mickey said.

"Makes what official?"

"That we are the two coolest guys in all of grade nine."

"How do you figure that?"

"Aside from our style and good looks, look around," he said, gesturing at the car.

"Yeah?"

"Think about it. You are the first, and so far only, grade nine kid in the entire school who has his license. Let's say we want to take out a couple of girls. We have a major advantage over everybody else. We can pick them up in a car, man. Everybody else has to have their mommy drive them or take a bus or a bike. Now which way do you think is better, car or public transit?"

He did have a point there.

"And nobody else in our grade can even try to get their license until next year because nobody else is old enough. Isn't it great that you flunked out last year?"

"That isn't exactly the way I looked at it." Not to mention how my parents had looked at it.

I still felt myself cringe a little bit when I thought about last year. School had never been easy for me—actually it had always been pretty hard—but last year it all just caught up with me. In grade school the teachers had always been helpful, sort of pushing me, offering extra help. Not last year. Grade nine hit me like a punch in the gut. Or more like a lot of punches in the gut. I had eight different teachers and I hardly knew their names, so it wasn't surprising that they didn't know me. Or care about me.

I tried. I really did try. But in the end I failed six of eight classes. I passed gym and technology. The rest just started badly and then got worse. The vice principal had tried to convince my parents that I should be transferred to another school, but nobody wanted that—especially me. In the end it was probably going to happen anyway, whether I liked it or not.

Then Miss Parsons stepped in. Miss Parsons was my guidance counselor. She went to bat for me and said she'd be my "mentor" and help me out. And all of this year she'd been there for me, checking on how I was doing, arranging for extra help. She was nice and I liked her. I trusted her.

I figured that doing grade nine for the second time would have made things half as hard. Instead it was twice as boring and almost as hard. So far I had passes in all eight courses, although in five of them—math, geography, history, English and biology—I was hanging in there by the skin of my teeth and getting marks in the low fifties. I didn't even know why I needed to take those courses. How would history help a guy become a good mechanic? The only history I would need to know was the history of the vehicle so I'd know when to do scheduled work.

In the other three courses—gym, technology and especially auto mechanics—I was pulling off aces. My marks were so high in those three that my overall average was 65. Maybe not great, but enough to keep everybody off my back.

"I bet you never thought that flunking out a year would be such an advantage!"

"Yeah, that's why I did it—so I'd be the oldest kid in grade nine," I said. "This was all part of my master plan."

"And a great master plan it was."

"And I want to thank you for all your help in reminding me I flunked out last year," I said.

"What?" Mickey asked. "Is this some sort of secret or something?"

"The only secret is why I don't just pound you out."

"Touchy, touchy."

He was right. I was touchy about it. It had been hard to stay in grade nine while everybody I knew—everybody who'd been in my class since kindergarten—moved on. At first I didn't know anybody in any of my classes, until I met Mickey. I guess I shouldn't have been so hard on him. He helped me feel at least like I was part of the grade and helped me make new friends. I still saw some of my old friends. I did take tech and gym with them. But it was different. Some of them treated me okay, but most treated me like I wasn't one of them anymore.

And then there were those kids—those jerks—who had never treated me well to begin with. You know the type. The kids with parents who had a little more money, or those kids who had better clothes or did well in school without trying hard. Why was it that some kids who had everything already always needed to point out how much better they were than you? It was a couple of those goofs who never missed a chance to remind me that I wasn't as smart as they were. If it wasn't for the fact that I couldn't afford to get suspended, I would have let them know that giving me a hard time wasn't a sign of brains—unless they wanted to wear those brains on the outside of their skulls. I would have just loved to smack them right in the—

"Look at that car!" Mickey exclaimed as a beautiful silver Acura glided by in the other direction. "That is one fantastic-looking car!"

"It's okay," I said, trying not to sound too impressed.

"It could probably blow the doors off this thing!" he said.

"Could not," I said. "Just because it looks good doesn't mean it has any guts under the hood."

"Doesn't mean that it doesn't," Mickey said.

"Take my word for it. I don't need to know what's under their hood because I know what's under our hood. This car can move."

"Are you saying this is the fastest thing on the road?" Mickey asked.

"Of course not. We're going to see some cars tonight that are out of this world. Just try not to be impressed by things that aren't impressive."

"You make it sound like I don't know nothing about cars," Mickey said defensively.

"Well…you don't."

"I don't know cars like you do, but I know cars," Mickey said. Up ahead of us the light turned red and I brought us to a stop.

"Like, look at the two cars across the way," Mickey said, motioning to the other side of the intersection. There were two cars—another Acura and a Camaro—sitting there side by side. They both revved their engines. I looked over at the lights in the other direction. The green gave way to a yellow and then a red. It would just be a couple of seconds and…the light turned to green and the two cars squealed away, leaving patches of rubber and smoke. The Camaro pulled away as they shot past. In my side-view mirror, the brake lights on both cars glowed as they closed down the race part-way down the block.

"That one went to the Camaro," I said.

"I'd like to see that car up close," Mickey said.

"You'll probably have a chance. Everybody always ends up in the parking lot of the Burger Barn sooner or later."

"Are we going there now?" Mickey asked.

"Later. I just want to cruise a little. Let's drive the strip a few times first."

Chapter Three

It seemed like every minute brought more traffic, an endless stream of cars on the road and people crowding the sidewalk. I'd done this strip along the sidewalk before, and in the passenger seat with my brother driving, but this was different. Way different.

As we sat at the light, I revved the engine ever so slightly.

"Do you think you can take 'em?" Mickey asked.

"Take who?"

He gestured toward the vehicle sitting beside us at the lights. It was a minivan with a woman the age of my mother at the wheel.

The light changed and I accelerated. The car jumped forward, leaving the minivan behind.

"All right, your first win!" Mickey laughed.

"That wasn't a race and I wasn't racing."

Up ahead, the next light turned red.

"Pull over to the curb lane!" Mickey exclaimed.

"Why?"

"Just do it!"

I checked my rearview mirror. The minivan hadn't managed to catch up. I switched lanes.

"Do you see what I see?" Mickey asked.

I looked all around and then checked out my mirrors. I saw lots of cars but nothing special.

"Right there at the lights, on the sidewalk."

We pulled up to the lights and I saw what Mickey had been excited about.

There, standing waiting for the lights to change, were two girls about our age—maybe a little bit older.

"They look like they're going the same way as us," Mickey said. "Maybe we should offer them a ride."

"Maybe we shouldn't."

"Maybe one of us hasn't got any guts or—"

"Maybe one of us should shut up," I said, cutting him off.

"What's it going to hurt to ask them?"

I didn't have an answer to that.

"What's the worst thing that can happen? They say no?"

Mickey rolled down his window. "Hey, girls!"

They didn't turn around. Either they hadn't heard him, or they had and were ignoring him.

"Hey, gorgeous!" he yelled out louder, and both of them turned around to face us. One of them actually was gorgeous. The other was—how could I say it politely?—not so gorgeous. They were all made-up and looked like they were out for a night on the town. They both held cans of pop, and one had a cigarette in her hand—yuck!

"So, girls, you want a ride?" Mickey called as he leaned out through the car's window.

The gorgeous one made a face like she'd just eaten something that tasted bad. She reached her arm back and pitched the can at the car. It clanked down on the hood, and the pop exploded up and onto the windshield!

Mickey had pulled his head into the car for protection. He leaned back out the window. "Does that mean no?" he asked.

The light changed and I gunned the engine to get us out of there.

Mickey started to laugh uncontrollably.

"You think that was funny?" I demanded.

"Of course it was funny."

"She didn't hit your car with a can!"

"Come on, how much damage could it have done?" he asked.

"Coke isn't good for a paint job."

"Who cares?" he asked. "Next week, after it's painted, it would have been a problem, but now?"

Of course he was right.

"Too bad, though," Mickey said. "Mine was really good-looking."

"What do you mean by that?" I asked.

"Isn't it obvious that I would have ended up with the great-looking one?"

I shook my head. "Mickey, sometimes."

"Sometimes what?"

"Nothing."

I downshifted and let the engine slow us down as we hit the traffic at the next light. It was impossible to drive very far or very fast without running into something, and I was trying to be extra careful. I couldn't imagine anything worse than getting in an accident.

25

"Now that's beautiful," Mickey said.

I looked over. It was obvious what he was referring to. Almost right beside us sat a beautiful, fully restored, top-of-the line, customized Mustang. I inched the car forward so we could pull up level with it. Behind the wheel was a girl—no, make that a woman. She had to be at least twenty and was as well-put-together as the car. Blonde hair, sunglasses perched on top of her head. I couldn't see what she was wearing, but her shoulders were bare.

"Just beautiful," Mickey said loudly enough for her to hear through the open window of her car. She turned and gave a little smile.

"Incredible body… great lines," Mickey continued. "I just love those older models. What year?" he asked.

"Sixty-seven," she said.

"Sixty-seven?" Mickey repeated, like he couldn't believe his ears. "Oh…the car." He paused. "I wasn't talking about the car."

I felt myself cringe and tried to sink as low into the seat as possible so she couldn't see me.

The woman suddenly started to laugh. "I'm afraid I'm a little old for you," she said. "But nice try."

A car honked from behind and I startled. I hadn't noticed the light change. I put the car into gear and drove away.

"Did you hear that?" Mickey beamed. "She said 'nice try'. If I was just a couple of years older, who knows what could have happened? Pull up beside her again," he ordered.

I put on my left turn signal and crossed over the lanes of oncoming traffic, pulling into a gas station.

"What are you doing?" he demanded.

"Getting some gas," I said. I pulled up at the pumps and climbed out of the car.

"But we can get gas later!" Mickey yelled as he jumped out of the car. "I have to convince her that I'm really eighteen!"

"Are we talking age or IQ points?"

"What?" he asked, not understanding my joke.

"We need it now," I said. That was a lie. We still had almost a quarter tank, but I didn't want to follow that woman. The only thing that could possibly lead to was more embarrassment.

"Come on, we can still catch her!"

"How cool do you think you'd look pushing the car if I ran out of gas?" I asked. I started pumping gas.

"Fine, so what if we let the woman of my dreams drive away," Mickey sighed.

"Don't worry. We can find her," I said.

"We can?"

"Sure," I said with a shrug. "She's probably going to the Burger Barn."

"How do you know that?"

"Where else would somebody with a hot car end up?" I asked.

"You're right," he said enthusiastically.

"I'll even let you buy me a burger."

"Why am I buying?"

"Because I'm paying for the gas."

Mickey looked up at the pump. The dollars kept rolling around and around and around.

"Do you want to pay for the gas instead?" I asked.

"Tell you what," Mickey said. "How about if I buy you some fries and a drink to go with that burger?"

Chapter Four

"This is unbelievable!" Mickey gushed.

"It's okay," I said, trying to sound cool and casual.

"Just okay?" he said as he gestured to the cars all around us in the parking lot. "For you this must be like dying and going to heaven."

"I guess it is a little bit better than okay," I admitted.

All around us, filling every spot in the Burger Barn parking lot, were some of the hottest cars in the city. There were Acuras and Hondas, North American muscle cars—Camaros, Vettes, Mustangs—and fancy Europeans like BMWs and Audis. It seemed like every car I'd ever drooled over was sitting here in the parking lot. Some of the cars had their hoods open, showing off their engines. Others were sitting there, idling away, so people could hear the music coming out from under the hood. Lots of people were sitting in their cars, but just as many were standing beside their vehicles. Sometimes you'd see somebody with a cloth, polishing up their paint job. There were also groups of people—mostly guys—all talking about the same thing, cars. This is where gear heads came to talk about the thing they loved.

"This is nothing compared to how I've seen it before," I said to Mickey.

"You're joking, right?"

"The hottest cars don't come out until later at night."

"That's hard to believe."

"Maybe I can get Andy to bring you along the next time he takes me."

"Your brother would do that?"

"If you promised to keep your mouth shut."

"I can do that," Mickey said.

"You can?"

"Well…I can try."

Andy said that Mickey had to learn to shut up sometimes. I didn't disagree.

I took the last sip from my Coke and tossed the container in the full garbage can. During the week this place was practically deserted, but every Friday and Saturday—especially when the weather was good—it was packed.

We walked up the line of parked cars. I listened in on conversations, looked at the engines and inhaled the smell of motors. Mickey was right—for me this was like heaven.

"So what happens now?" Mickey asked.

I looked at my watch. "What happens is that we better get going."

"I meant what happens for everybody else? Do they just sit here all night? Or is there going to be some action?"

"There'll be some action."

The drivers didn't just bring their cars here to show off. This wasn't just about what a car looked like. It was about how it could perform. I knew that before the night was over cars, would start slipping away—alone or in pairs—to reassemble at an agreed spot. Then they'd be testing each other. They'd be street racing.

"If we stay here, will we get to see somebody race?" Mickey asked.

"Here?" I asked in disbelief.

"I didn't mean in the parking lot," he said. "I mean around here."

"Too much heat. Haven't you noticed the police?"

"I saw a couple of squad cars pass by," he said.

Actually, one of them had even taken a slow pass through the parking lot.

"You might see some guys fooling

around—you know, revving their engines or even doing a jump start from the lights—but nothing serious. That happens way north of here on deserted roads in the country."

"They drive all that way?" Mickey asked.

"Of course they do. Do you think they'd be stupid enough to race right here? If the cops didn't get you, you'd still risk smashing into something or somebody."

"But what about those two cars we saw earlier tonight?"

"They just jumped off the line and then shut it down. They weren't really racing.... at least, not racing very far."

"And that's okay?"

"Maybe not okay, but people do it."

"Does your brother street race?" Mickey asked.

I didn't answer.

"I guess that means yes."

"You didn't hear it from me," I said. Andy would never admit it to me, but I knew. You didn't invest that much time and money in a car unless you planned on letting it loose every now and again.

But I also knew my brother. I knew that he would try to be as safe and responsible as he could be. Somehow that struck me as a pretty strange thought—being safe and responsible while doing something dangerous and irresponsible. Now I was starting to think like my parents. Maybe it was time to give my head a good shake.

"I wish we could stay longer," Mickey said.

I looked at my watch again. It was definitely time to leave. It wouldn't be smart to be late if I wanted to borrow Andy's car again.

"Let's go," I said.

We walked along the row of parked cars. I was parked in the far corner of the back lot. I'd parked there because I figured the front lot would be full, but also because it just didn't seem right to park out front. It wasn't my car, and it wasn't finished. It would be up to my brother to decide when it could be parked up front.

"You were wrong," Mickey said.

"Wrong about what?"

"She wasn't here."

"She? Who?"

"The girl, the woman, in the Mustang. She wasn't here."

"She'll probably be here later. Just what were you planning to say to her if she was here?"

"I wasn't going to be saying anything. At least, not at first. I figured she'd be coming up and talking to me."

I laughed. "You really do live in a fantasy world, don't you?"

He shook his head. "You just don't understand women at all."

"And you do?"

"That is correct. And that is why we make such a good team. You have the car and I have the cool."

"The car is real," I said, pointing into the corner where it was parked. "The cool is something I've yet to see."

Chapter Five

We slowly cruised along the strip. This would be our last pass of the night as we drove home.

"What do you want to do for the rest of the night?" Mickey asked.

"I don't know. Maybe watch a movie. See who's around and what they're doing," I suggested.

"Whatever it is, it's going to be boring compared to this. Do you think your brother would take us along with him tonight?"

"No way, he's going on a date."

"Oh…I thought he was coming back out here to cruise."

"He doesn't come here all the time."

Up ahead the light turned red and I came to a stop at the line. A black BMW stopped beside us. I looked over. The passenger-side window glided down.

"How's it going, Jakey?"

"It was going just fine," I muttered. Of all the people to run into, he was the last I wanted to meet. I'd known Luke since grade three. He was sort of a jerk back then, and he'd become a bigger jerk every year since. I think he actually got a charge out of me failing the year before.

"I don't get to see you much these days, what with you still being in grade nine." I felt myself tense up.

"Well, it's nice to see you out here with all your friends," I said.

"My friends? There's nobody in the car but me." He scowled as he realized that I'd just insulted him.

"And I see you're with one of your little friends," he said. "Too bad you won't be together next year when he goes on to grade ten and you stay behind in grade nine again. Maybe you can make some more little friends. Who would have thought that grade nine was going to be the longest three years of your life, huh?"

"Why don't you shut up!" I snapped.

Before he could answer, the light changed and I drove away. He quickly caught up and sped by. The light up ahead turned red. He stopped at the line. I pulled in beside him. He looked over and glared at me. "It's easy to see who has the better car."

"It's easy to see that your daddy has a better car!" I snapped.

"So, is your car as slow as you?" he asked.

I had to fight the urge to jump out of the car and pound the snot out of him.

"Did you get that joke or do you want me to explain it to you?" he asked.

"The only joke here is you and that hunk of shiny steel you think is a car!" I snapped. Maybe there was only one way to shut him up. "Let's see if either you or your car has any guts!"

"All right," Mickey said. "All right."

I tightened my grip on the steering wheel. I pushed down on the accelerator and the engine revved.

The road up ahead was clear and open.

"Turn up the music," I said.

"What?" Mickey asked.

"Turn up the music!"

He leaned over and turned up the volume. "Louder!"

He turned it up again. I kept my eye on the other light. It was still green—no, it changed to yellow! It would only be a couple more seconds. I heard him revving his car. I didn't look over. Now I stared straight at the red light, waiting for it to turn green. I let up slightly on the clutch, revved the engine and double-checked I was in first gear.

"Come on, come on." The light changed to green. I popped the clutch and stomped down on the accelerator. The car jumped forward and I felt myself being pressed back into the seat. The sound of squealing tires, engines roaring, the CD blaring and Mickey yelling deafened me. The car rocketed across the intersection. I glanced at the side-view mirror...he'd hardly gotten off the line and I was pulling farther and farther away! I pushed down on the brakes. This race was over and done.

"You blew his doors off!" Mickey screamed. "No contest, man! No contest!"

As I looked at Mickey, the BMW shot past in a black blur.

"What an idiot!" I yelled. "The race is over and he lost! Look at him keep going."

"Look out!" Mickey screamed.

At the next intersection the BMW plowed into the side of a silver car turning left onto the strip. There was an explosion of smoke and metal parts.

"You're going to hit it!" Mickey yelled. I cranked the wheel hard to the right, almost jumping the sidewalk, and just squeezed by the two tangled cars. The car bucked and rocked. I took my foot off the gas and brake and struggled to bring it back under control.

"Oh, wow, wow, wow," Mickey muttered. He turned around in his seat. I looked in my rearview mirror, but couldn't make things out clearly.

"What happened?" I screamed.

"He hit that car…it was turning left…he hit it!"

"Can you see how bad it is?" I demanded.

"Bad, bad, really bad."

I slowed the car and we came to a stop at the side of the road. The accident was at least a full block behind us now.

"What are you doing?" Mickey demanded.

"We have to go back," I said.

"We have to get out of here!" Mickey yelled.

"But we have to go back and see if everybody's okay."

"Do you know how much trouble we can get into…how much trouble *you* can get into?"

I hadn't thought about anything.

"We have to get out of here. There's nothing we can do. Besides, there are already people there to help and to call the police. There's nothing we can do but get in trouble."

I hesitated.

"Go! Get out of here!"

I got the car moving. I had one eye on the road in front and the other on my rearview mirror, trying to see the accident. I saw flashing red lights behind me in the distance. For a split second I took my foot off the accelerator. Then I pressed down harder, picked up speed and took a quick left turn.

Chapter Six

We drove along without saying a word. I leaned over and turned off the CD.

"That was close," Mickey said.

"Close? They hit."

"Close for us, I mean, and close only counts in horseshoes and hand grenades."

"What?" I demanded.

"A joke. A bad joke."

"I don't want to hear an—" I stopped as I

heard the sound of a siren. Were they coming after us? Up ahead I saw the lights coming down the road toward us. I eased my foot off the gas even though I hadn't been speeding. The lights got bigger and the siren louder and louder and then the police car shot past us. It was probably going to the accident.

I sighed in relief.

"I don't know what you're worried about," Mickey said. "You didn't do anything wrong."

"I was street racing with him!"

"Before the accident happened."

"Like five seconds before the accident happened!"

"Five seconds, five minutes, five months... you weren't racing him when the accident happened, right?"

"No," I admitted.

"And if he hadn't been such an idiot and kept racing, then it wouldn't have happened. The accident is his fault...or maybe the fault of the guy who cut in front of him...but it's not your fault."

I didn't know what to say. Maybe Mickey was right. But I still thought I should have stopped.

"I think it's against the law to leave the scene of an accident," I said.

"But you weren't in the accident. You were just driving by it. I bet you there were dozens and dozens of cars driving by in the other direction before the police arrived. Do you think all of them stopped?"

"Of course not, but they weren't almost involved in the accident," I argued.

"Almost is the important word. You weren't involved because you drove so well to get around it. They should give you some sort of driving award for not hitting those cars."

Again I didn't know what to say. Everything he said made sense. He was right. Or at least, I wanted him to be right.

I turned onto my street. I felt safe. I slowed down and went to pull into the driveway when I saw my brother standing there. He looked annoyed.

"What time is it?" I asked.

"A couple of minutes after ten."

"Great, just great," I muttered. I pulled into the driveway and turned to Mickey. "Not a word about what happened. Not to him. Not to anybody. Understand?"

"I guess so."

"No guessing!" I snapped. "Do you understand?"

"Yeah. Sure. Nothing."

We climbed out of the car.

"Tick tock," Andy said, tapping his watch as he walked up to the car.

"I'm really sorry," I apologized.

"Not as sorry as you're going to be if I'm late to pick up Natalie. She can turn ugly really fast if I'm not on time."

"Sorry," I repeated.

Andy looked like he was studying me.

"What's wrong?" I asked.

"That's what I'd like to know."

"What do you mean?"

"You didn't say anything about how easy it would be for Natalie to turn ugly or something like that."

"Why would I say—"

"You always take shots at Natalie. Why not now? What happened?"

"Nothing happened!" I protested.

"Did you do something to the car?" he questioned. "Did you break something or hit something or—"

"I didn't hit anything, honest!"

"Then what's that?" he demanded, pointing at the hood.

"What?"

"Right there on the hood. Is that a dent?"

Andy reached over and touched the hood. That was the place where the Coke can had hit.

"And it's sticky? Why is it sticky?"

I looked over at Mickey. He was studying his shoes.

"Somebody spilled a pop on it," I said.

"And you didn't wash it off?"

"I was going to."

"You *are* going to! Right now! Do you know what Coke can do to a car's paint?"

"I know, but I didn't think it mattered because it's getting painted next—"

"It eats into the primer coat, and if you don't wash it off, then the next coat won't stick right. Get a bucket right now."

"I'll help you," Mickey said. "It was my fault."

"You spilled the pop?" Andy demanded.

"No, not me!" Mickey said, holding his hands in front of him like he was afraid my brother was going to pop him or was surrendering before he had a chance to get hit.

"And how did a pop spilling cause a dent in the hood?" my brother demanded.

My mind scrambled, looking for an answer that wasn't coming.

"Forget it!" he said. "I probably don't even want to know."

"I'll fix it," I said. "I promise."

"That's right, you will fix it. First thing tomorrow morning. The car is scheduled at the paint shop on Monday. The filler has to have enough time to dry before then."

"I'll even do it tonight if you want."

"Tonight I need the car for my date with …oh, great," he muttered.

For an instant I wondered what was wrong. Then I saw the answer as Natalie's car pulled into the driveway.

"This isn't good," he said. "I'm going to tell her the car wouldn't start and that's why I'm late. When I get back, that car better be washed down and the dent fixed or there's going to be a few more dents. And I'm not talking about the car, if you get my drift."

I understood him perfectly.

Natalie got out of the car and loudly slammed the door.

"Natalie!" Andy said as he walked down the driveway. "You look beautiful tonight. I'm so sorry I'm late! I had a little bit of trouble with the car."

"I don't want to hear about that car!" she shrieked.

She had a high-pitched whiny voice that sounded like fingernails on a chalkboard.

"Sometimes I think you care more about that car than you do about me!" she continued.

"Of course I don't!" Andy protested. "Did I mention how fantastic you look tonight?"

"As opposed to how I usually look? Is that what you're saying?" she demanded.

"No, of course not! You always look fantastic. Tonight you just look more fantastic than usual."

I was thinking that I didn't know what my brother saw in her, and then I remembered. She stood there in her skintight pants, high heels and low-cut top. What I didn't understand was how he could think anybody was good-looking enough to be worth all the grief he took from her.

Andy continued to alternate between apologizing and flattering Natalie as they climbed into her car and drove away.

Chapter Seven

As soon as I was sure that they'd driven out of view, I started up the car and pulled it into the garage. It felt good to get it into the garage and out of sight. I grabbed a bucket and squirted in some soap. Next I filled the bucket with water from the hose. I took a sponge, dipped it in the soapy water, wrung it out and then rubbed down the hood.

"You planning on washing the whole car, or what?" Mickey asked.

"Just the whole hood."

"This certainly isn't how I figured on spending the rest of the night, washing a car and doing bodywork."

"It won't be the whole night. Actually I can't even do the bodywork until this is completely dry."

"You going to use a blow-dryer?" Mickey joked.

"Sort of."

I walked over to the workbench and grabbed a heat lamp. I set it up on the hood.

"So now we're going to stand here and watch it dry?" Mickey asked.

"No. Now we're going to get a couple of bikes and go for a ride," I explained.

"A ride? Where to?" Mickey asked.

"Back to the strip," I said.

"What? I don't think we should do that."

"Why not?" I asked.

"I don't know why not, I just don't think we should."

"I need to know what happened. You don't have to come if you don't want to."

"I don't want to," he said. "But that doesn't mean I'm not coming."

I grabbed my bike. "You can take my sister's bike."

"I'm not going to ride your little sister's bike!" he protested. "What if somebody sees me?"

"Mickey, just stop trying to act so cool. Get on the bike. Let's go."

He looked like he was going to say something, but he didn't. We walked the bikes out of the garage and I closed the big door behind us. I was happy to keep the car completely out of sight.

We rode along the street and then cut down a pathway. There were walkways throughout the neighborhood that cut between streets. As we pedaled along, I kept thinking about the accident. Was anybody hurt? Was it my fault? Had anybody seen me? And what sort of trouble could I get in if they found out Luke was racing with me before the accident? I pushed down harder on the pedals and tried to push the thoughts out of my mind. The bike picked up speed, but the thoughts stayed stuck in my head.

We stopped well behind the people who lined the sidewalk, watching, staring, gawking at the accident. I got off the bike and leaned it against a telephone pole. Mickey put my sister's bike beside it.

As we got closer, I understood why the crowd was so large. The two cars—the black BMW and a silver SUV—looked like they'd been welded together in a single piece of tangled, smashed metal. If it weren't for the difference in the colors of the two vehicles, I wouldn't have been able to tell where one started and the other one ended.

There were emergency vehicles lining the street: three police cars, a couple of ambulances, five...no, six tow trucks and a big fire truck. The lights on top of all of the vehicles were circling around, flashing, bathing the scene in a series of lights, like some sort of dance or party.

A fireman was hosing down the road, washing away gas or oil. Or blood. Another fireman had a broom and was sweeping away larger pieces of the cars. There were two policemen, both wearing orange reflective vests, directing traffic. Only one lane was open and traffic was backed up for blocks. As cars passed, they slowed down and drivers and passengers gawked at the accident.

"Looks bad," Mickey said to a woman standing at the edge of the crowd. "Was anybody hurt?"

"Everybody was hurt," she said. "The one ambulance has already gone. The one with the driver of the black car."

"How did he look?" I asked anxiously.

"Not good. He wasn't moving."

"What do you mean? Is he dead?"

"If he had been they wouldn't have been putting him in an ambulance and shooting off with the lights on."

"Thank goodness," I said.

"Of course, that doesn't mean anything. Lord knows how he is now." She turned to look at me. "He seemed about your age. Do you know him?"

"No!" I protested. "I was just worried, that's all. Do you know how many people were involved in the accident?"

"Three. The boy in the car and a couple in the SUV."

"I guess they weren't hurt very badly because the ambulances are still here," Mickey said.

"The ambulances are still here because they can't get the one woman out of the car," she said. "She's trapped inside."

"Trapped?"

"The fire department is going to have to cut her out. They're getting ready to use the Jaws of Life."

"The what?" Mickey asked.

"Watch," the woman said.

Almost on cue, two of the firemen pressed a large machine against the side of the SUV.

They began to cut through the roof of the car. It was like some sort of combination chain saw and gigantic can opener. It sliced through the metal, and the fireman peeled back the side and roof of the car. They turned off the machine and two paramedics raced forward. They removed a woman from the passenger seat. The side of her head was bandaged and there was something wrong with her leg…it was sticking out at a strange angle.

"She looks okay, I guess," Mickey said.

"That's where the BMW hit, right into the side of the SUV, right into the passenger door."

A man—his head all bandaged as well—rushed to her side as they placed her on a stretcher.

"I can't be sure," the woman said, "but she looks pregnant."

The sick feeling that had been growing in my stomach got worse.

A man standing just in front of us turned around. "I heard the kid was street racing."

"That's awful. A couple just out for dinner, minding their own business doing nothing wrong and this happens."

"I wonder what happened to the other car," the man said.

"What other car?" the woman asked.

"The car the BMW was racing."

"Did you see another car?" she asked. My heart rose up into my throat.

"Naw. Just figured. Nobody races by themselves, that's all."

I stumbled away from the crowd. Mickey followed after me.

"You okay?" he asked.

I nodded weakly.

"You look awful," he said. "You're all white."

"We gotta go. Now."

Chapter Eight

I sat bolt upright, my heart racing. I looked around. I was in my bed. In my bedroom. It was light, which meant it was morning.

My brother was in his bed on the other side of the room. He must have come in pretty late. I was awake until after three in the morning—I couldn't stop thinking about the accident—and when I finally closed my eyes, he still wasn't in. I guess when I did fall asleep I was really asleep because I hadn't even heard him come in. He was gently snoring and there was a smile on his face. He always had a smile on his face the morning after a date with Natalie.

I was completely awake. The scene on the street—the tangled metal of the cars, the police, firemen, the ambulances, everything—all seemed like a dream. A nightmare. I needed to know more about the accident.

I climbed out of bed and quietly left the room. The whole house was silent. As I came down the stairs I could hear the clock ticking on the mantel. It was a few minutes before 8:00. That was way too early to be up on a Saturday morning. Everybody else was obviously still asleep, and in my brother's case would stay asleep for hours to come.

I went to the front door and opened it just wide enough for me to reach out and get the paper from the mailbox, but not so wide that anyone outside would see me in nothing but my boxers.

I grabbed the paper and let the door close as I retreated inside. I put the folded paper under my arm. I wanted to look—especially at the front page—but I didn't want to look even harder. I was afraid of what I might see.

I sat down at the kitchen table, took a deep breath and opened up the paper. There on the front cover was a gigantic picture of some guys, and a headline that said "Peace Slipping Away in the Middle East." How could something that didn't exist slip away?

I was relieved to see that there was absolutely nothing on the front page about the accident. I turned the page and scanned the stories. Nothing there either. Quickly I went page by page through the whole first section. Nothing. I put aside the sports pages and the classifieds. It wouldn't be in either of those sections. The last section was titled City. That's where it could be. Slowly I looked from story to story, page by page. There was nothing about the accident. How could that be possible? I worked my way backward through the whole section. Nothing.

I didn't know whether I should feel relieved or disappointed. Instead I felt both. It was like the accident never happened—which I knew was wrong. Maybe it hadn't been as big or bad an accident as I thought and I was just overreacting.

Then I thought of something else. The accident took place pretty late in the evening. Maybe the newspaper had already been put together and printed before the accident could make it into the papers. That would just mean I wouldn't know anything more until Sunday's paper came out.

The phone rang. I jumped out of my seat. Who could be calling this early in the morning? What if it was the police? Somebody had seen me racing and had written down my license plate number and now they were calling and—the phone rang again. Would the police call or would they just show up at the door? The phone rang a third time.

Police or no police, I had to answer it before it woke everyone up. I grabbed the phone.

"He…hello," I stuttered.

"Jake?"

"Yes?"

"It's me, Mickey."

"Mickey…what are you doing calling so early?"

"Did you see it?"

"See what?" I asked anxiously.

"The TV news flash. The accident was on TV."

"You're kidding. It was on TV?"

"Yeah, they made it into a big story. I couldn't sleep, so I was up watching the tube and then it came on," he said. "It interrupted the late movie."

"What did they say?"

"They talked about the people that were injured. There were three people hurt, but only two of them were hospitalized."

I took a deep breath. "Luke and…and…"

"The woman. The pregnant woman. The reporter said they had to keep her in for observation because they wondered if the force of the accident would cause her to lose the baby."

I felt my legs go soft. If I hadn't been sitting down, I thought I might have fallen over.

"What else did they say?"

"They interviewed some cop and he said they were looking for another car," Mickey said.

Now I knew I would have fallen down.

"But there's good news," Mickey said.

"How can any of this be good?"

"They said they're looking for a white car."

"White? But my brother's car isn't white."

"I know that. I think those patches of primer paint made them think it was white. And by Monday, because of the paint job, the car is going to be even less white…it's going to be red."

"That's right," I said.

"Isn't that good news?" Mickey asked.

"I guess. But what if somebody saw my license plate?"

"Do you have a cop at your front door?" Mickey asked.

"No…I don't think so…I just peeked out the door and—"

"You don't or you'd know it," Mickey said, cutting me off. "And if anybody got your license plate, then there'd be a whole squad of cops there already."

"I guess you're right," I said. "Although I really didn't do anything wrong…right?"

"I'm afraid you're wrong now and were right last night," he said.

"What does that mean?"

"The cop said that cars that see an accident are supposed to stay around to give a report. Especially if they were somehow involved."

"Involved," I said. "Like we were involved. Do you think I should . . . I should call?"

"Only if you're an idiot!" he snapped. "They didn't see you. They don't know who you are. Just don't do anything."

"I guess you're right," I said.

"I know I'm right. Calling can only get us in trouble."

I didn't answer. Somehow it didn't seem right. There were two people in the hospital—one of them a pregnant woman who might lose her baby—and while I hadn't hit the other car, it was still my fault. Sort of. Maybe. I just didn't know.

"So, we both keep our mouths shut. Agreed?" Mickey asked.

"Yeah. Agreed."

"So, you want to do something today?" Mickey asked. His voice was cheery and happy, like he'd suddenly forgotten what we were just talking about.

"I don't know," I said. "I have things to do today. I'll see you tomorrow or Monday at school."

Chapter Nine

"What's wrong with you?" Andy asked.

"What do you mean?"

"Are you sick or something?"

"I'm not sick."

"Then why didn't you go out last night?"

"I don't always go out."

"You almost always go out on Saturday nights."

"But not always."

"And now you've been moping around the house all day," he continued.

"I don't even know what moping means, and even if I did, I wasn't doing it, so shut up," I said.

He shook his head slowly. "Sometimes I can't believe you're my brother. I've got to check with Mom. Either you were dropped on your head when you were a baby or we adopted you. There's no way we're related."

"Why don't you shut up or else I'll—"

"You'll what?" He started moving around the room like a boxer, bobbing and weaving and tossing pretend punches. "You may be getting bigger, but I'm always going to be your bigger brother," he said.

"Correction. You'll always be my older brother, but in about two years I'll be the bigger brother and looking down on you."

"Speaking of looking down, where's the Mouse?"

My brother always called Mickey, the Mouse.

"He's probably at home," I answered.

"So the Mouse is in his house. I think I could make that into a rap lyric or a Dr. Seuss story. Something like, 'Do you want that mouse in your house? Oh, no, I don't want that mouse in my house.' That would sell. Any idiot can write a kids' book."

"If being an idiot helps, you could be one fine writer," I said.

"So, seriously, why have you just been hanging around all day?"

"I've been studying," I lied.

"Studying what, the TV and newspaper …and when did you start reading anything except the sports section and comics?" he asked, gesturing to the paper strewn around the floor at my feet.

"I read other parts of the paper," I argued. "I'm not the one who only looks at the Sunshine Girl picture on page three."

"That is the best part of the whole paper. You'd understand that if you started hanging around with Minnie instead of Mickey Mouse," Andy said.

I tried hard not to laugh, but I couldn't help myself. The guy was funny. As big brothers went, he was pretty good.

"You know, I wouldn't mind the Mouse if he'd learn to just shut his mouth sometimes," my brother said. "I'd hate to trust a secret to that guy."

I felt a chill go up my spine.

"Too bad about that kid, huh?"

"Kid, what kid?" I asked suspiciously.

"The kid in that car...the story's right there in the paper...you read it, didn't you?"

I hesitated. What should I say?

"The kid who crashed his father's BMW. You were sitting here when it came on the six o'clock news, remember?"

"Oh, yeah, that's right."

"What was his name?"

"Um...Luke."

"He's sixteen, like you. Do you know him?"

Again I hesitated.

"It said that he goes to your school."

"He's a grade ahead of me," I said.

"So you do know him."

"Yeah. We've been in the same class before."

"I thought that name was familiar. He ever been to the house here?"

"Before. A long time before, like when we were in grade four or three," I admitted. Back then we'd been friends, sort of.

"What did it say in the paper about what happened?" Andy asked.

"Why are you so interested?"

He shrugged. "It has to do with cars. Why aren't you more interested?"

"I am interested. I'm just not obsessed."

"So tell me, what did you read?" he asked.

"It doesn't say much. It just says he was racing…at least, they think he was racing."

"Of course he was racing. Look at the picture," he said as he picked up the paper and pointed at it.

I didn't need to see the picture to know what it looked like. I had a clear, vivid picture locked in my head.

"Cars don't get this tangled unless there's a lot of speed involved, and it wouldn't have been coming from that SUV hanging the left-hand turn. The other car just got away, that's all."

"Other car?" I asked.

"The car he was racing."

I tried not to show any expression on my face. "Oh, yeah, the police are looking for a white car that was seen driving away." I paused. "What happens if they catch the guy?"

"He could be in big trouble." Andy said.

"But he wasn't in the accident. He didn't cause the accident!"

"How would you know that?" he asked.

"Well…I know he wasn't in the accident because there were only two cars, right?" I asked.

"Either way, he was racing."

"What if he wasn't racing right then?"

"What do you mean?" Andy looked confused.

"Suppose they were racing before the accident…like a couple of blocks before the accident, and the one guy shut it down?"

"And the second guy just kept on racing?" my brother asked.

"Yeah. Exactly. What would happen to the guy in the white car if it happened like that?"

"I'm not sure. Maybe nothing. I don't really know," he said. "I can't decide if that guy was really lucky or really unlucky."

"He must be lucky if he didn't get involved in the accident," I said.

"Or unlucky to be there in the first place."

I had to admit to myself that I did feel a lot more unlucky than I did lucky. "Have you ever street raced?" I'd never asked him that question that directly before.

Andy didn't answer, but one side of his mouth curled into a smirk.

"Have you?" I persisted.

"This better stay between you and me," he said as he lowered his voice.

"Then you have?"

He nodded his head. "I've had my share, but I've never been stupid enough to race on a crowded street with people and police all around. That friend of yours—"

"He's not a friend of mine!" I snapped.

"That guy was an idiot for doing what he did. How's he going to live with the fact that he may have killed a kid."

"A kid?"

"A baby. The baby in that woman's stomach."

"She lost the baby?" I gasped. I'd read the newspaper article four or five times and watched the news on TV, and it hadn't said anything about her having lost the—

He shrugged. "I don't know, but if she did, how could he live with that…that is if he lives. I heard he's pretty badly hurt."

The newspaper had said that he was in the intensive care unit in critical but stable condition.

But if he did make it, how could he live with himself if he killed that baby? And more important, how could I live with it? I had to find out more about what had happened. Even if what I found out wasn't good, I had to know.

Chapter Ten

I walked through the lobby of the hospital. With the carpets on the floor, and stores and coffee places lining the walls, it didn't feel like a hospital. It didn't smell like a hospital either. It just smelled like coffee. I pulled the lid off my coffee—my two-dollar-and-seventy-five cent fancy coffee—and took a sip. I figured that sip was worth about thirty-five cents.

I looked around me. This place reminded me more of a mall than a hospital. I guess if you had to be in a hospital, this was a pretty good hospital to be at. Not that I really wanted to be in any hospital. But I didn't have much of a choice.

I'd started off for school, but I found myself drawn in this direction. Now that I was here, what was I supposed to do next?

I walked up to the information desk. I waited in line as the woman at the desk helped the people in front of me, giving room numbers or directions. Then it was my turn. I hesitated.

"Um, why don't you go first," I said to the older woman standing right behind me.

"Oh, thank you," she said as she stepped forward. "Such a polite young man," she said to the woman behind the counter.

Polite had less to do with it than scared and confused. What was I supposed to say or ask?

"How I can help you?" the woman behind the counter asked.

I looked up. It was my turn. I guessed I could just let somebody else go ahead of me, but that was going to get old fast. I stepped forward.

"I was hoping to get some information," I said.

"Then you're definitely in the right place. Do you want to know about a patient?"

"Yes, a patient. Luke…Luke Johnson."

She punched away at the computer sitting on the counter.

"There we are," she said. "He's in room 2121." She pointed down at a map laminated onto the counter. "This is where we are, and you follow this corridor, take the elevator to the second floor. You turn left and—"

"No. I didn't want to visit him!" I said, cutting her off.

"You didn't?" she asked. She sounded confused.

"No." I had to come up with an answer. It did seem strange. "You know, I don't want to disturb him if he's really not doing good. I just wanted to know how he is," I explained.

"I'm afraid I can't tell you that," she said.

"But I can," said a man's voice from behind me.

I turned around. There were a man and woman standing there. "I'm Luke's uncle," the man said. "And this is his aunt. Are you a friend of Luke's?"

"Um, yeah."

"You'll be happy to know that he's doing better," the woman said.

"That's great!" I exclaimed. "I'm so glad to hear he's going to be all right."

The two exchanged concerned looks. "I think it's still a little early to say that," the man said.

"He's doing better, but he's still in the intensive care unit," the woman explained. "At least he's conscious now."

"Conscious?" I asked.

"Awake," the woman explained. "He was in a coma."

"A coma!" That was serious.

"He sustained a pretty bad head injury," said Luke's aunt.

"And according to his mother—she's my sister," the man said, "he still has almost no memory of the accident."

"He doesn't?" That might mean he had no memory of me.

"No," he said. "Actually, rather than stand here talking, why don't we head for the room? We didn't remember the number, but I over-heard the woman tell you it was 2121."

"Yeah, that's what she said, but I wasn't going to go up."

"You weren't?" the woman asked.

"I don't want to disturb him, or any-body…you know it's not like I'm family," I tried to explain.

"You won't be disturbing Luke. He's prob-ably sleeping," the man said. "That's how the brain heals itself after a bad injury. And I know it would mean so much to my sister to know Luke has such good friends. Not only will it not disturb anybody, I'm sure it will bring comfort."

"I don't know," I said. What was I going to do?

"Well I do. I insist you come with us."

I was going to argue, when the woman took me by the arm. "Come on," she said. I felt completely helpless to resist. What had I gotten myself into?

As I was escorted along the corridor, I thought I understood how a prisoner felt as he was walking to the electric chair. Maybe I could make a break for it, run out a door or into the washroom or—there was nothing I could do. I could just hope that he was asleep or that I was part of the accident he didn't remember.

"Here we are," the man said. "Room 2121."

We walked in the door. Luke's mother—I recognized her from a long time ago—jumped out of a chair, rushed over and threw her arms around them. She was crying. A man who had been standing by the bed came over and shook hands and they all said hello to each other.

I felt stupid standing there by myself at the door. Maybe this was the time for me to just slip out. "We brought along one of Luke's friends," the uncle said. "This is... this is..."

"Jake!" Luke's mother exclaimed. "It's been years since we've seen you! It's so good to see you!" She turned to her husband. "You remember Jake, don't you?"

"I think I do," he said, although the look on his face told me that he didn't. But then again, why should he remember me? I hadn't been over to their house for five or six years, and even back then I didn't go over very often. I was sure I looked different than I had then.

"It's a shame Luke is sleeping," his mother said. "If you'd been here a half hour ago he was awake."

"How is he doing?" Luke's uncle asked.

"The broken arm and the face are not serious," Mrs. Johnson said.

I looked over at Luke for the first time. The side of his face was all raw and bruised and his arm was in a cast. It certainly appeared serious to me.

"The part we're worried about is the head injury," she continued.

"Head injuries are serious," Luke's aunt agreed.

"How is he doing?" his uncle asked.

"A bit better. He's still mostly sleeping and his talk is slow—he can't find some words—and he has practically no memory of the whole day of the accident, but the doctor says she thinks he'll make a complete recovery."

"Thank goodness," I said, the words escaping my mouth before I'd even realized I'd said them.

"That's what we're all saying," his mother said. "And that's so kind of you to feel that way, so kind of you to come."

Kindness had nothing to do with it, but what could I say?

"The doctor said that as his brain heals he might regain full memory of the accident. We have so many questions, so many things that just don't make sense."

I could probably answer all of their questions right now if I wanted to. I had my own unanswered question. What would happen if he remembered that I was the guy in the other car?

"You're the only one of his friends to come, so far," his mother continued.

Unless things had changed dramatically this past year, he really didn't have a lot of friends.

"They'll probably come tonight, after school," Mr. Johnson said. He then turned to me. "You're not in school today?"

"Um, I thought it was okay to miss a couple of classes," I said. "A couple of classes won't hurt."

"You're right," Mrs. Johnson said. "Or even a couple of days. Unfortunately, Luke is going to miss a lot more than that. It could be months before he can go back to school."

"Maybe the rest of the year," Mr. Johnson said. "I think we pretty well have to write off this whole year. He was struggling before the accident, and now?" he said and shrugged. "I think the year is lost."

I knew that Luke wasn't a great student, but I didn't think he was having that much trouble.

"I think it's premature to look that far into the future, or to think that negatively," his mother argued. "Maybe the school can give him some extra help and we can hire a tutor and he can get notes from his classmates. Jake, do you and Luke share any classes?"

I shook my head. "Not this year. I'm not even in the same grade," I said, surprising myself. "I'm still in grade nine."

"Oh, I didn't know that," his father said.

"Luke doesn't talk a lot about school or things. Typical teenager," his mother said.

"It's good to know that if he has to repeat the year he'll have at least one friend in the same grade," his father said.

I was about to ask who that one friend was, when I realized he meant me. Before I could think of anything else to say, I heard a raspy voice.

"Hi."

It was Luke! He was awake. They all rushed to his bed and gave him hugs and asked him questions. When he spoke, his voice was hardly audible.

"And look who's here," his mother said, stepping aside so he could see me.

"Jake?" he asked, his voice soft and quivery.

"Yeah…hi, Luke," I said. I swallowed hard.

"You came to see me?" he asked.

"Yeah, to see if you were okay."

He hesitated, and from the look on his face it seemed like he really didn't understand what I'd said.

"I'm…I'm…going to be okay." He turned his head toward his mother. "I'm going to be okay…right?"

"That's what the doctors all say," she said and gave his arm a squeeze. "You're going to be just fine."

He nodded his head ever so slightly. "And everybody's going to be okay…right?"

"Everybody. The woman in the other

car is going to be just fine. Her and her newborn baby."

"She gave birth?" I asked, and then realized that maybe I shouldn't have said anything. "I'd read in the paper that she was pregnant."

"She was nine months pregnant. The accident caused her to go into labor a few days early, but she and the baby are both just fine," Luke's father said.

"Although I don't know how that poor woman is going to take care of a baby on a broken leg," Luke's mother said.

"She'll do just fine," his father said. "The baby's father is there to help."

Mrs. Johnson laughed. "I remember just how much help certain fathers were."

"I better get going," I said.

"Thank you so much for coming," Luke's mother said. To my complete surprise she came over and gave me a big hug. "Please tell all his friends that he's doing just fine and if they want to visit they can."

"I can do that," I said. I turned and went to leave.

"Jake?" Luke called out.

I stopped and turned around.

"Thanks...thanks for coming."

"You're welcome," I mumbled and then retreated out of the room. How grateful would they all be if they knew I was driving the other car?

Chapter Eleven

I looked anxiously at my watch. It said I still had three minutes until the bell rang to start afternoon classes. But I could never trust my watch to be in tune with the school clocks. Judging from the thinning crowds in the hall, the bell might ring any second.

Missing the whole morning wasn't good—especially when I didn't have a reason—but I could probably intercept the automated call home reporting me missing and delete it from the answering machine before my parents could hear it.

Being late for class would be harder because I'd have to face a real live teacher and explain myself. In this case, my math teacher. He was not one of my favorites, and the feeling was mutual. If it wasn't for the fact that it was math and I couldn't afford to cut that class, I might just have gone to the cafeteria and taken another spare.

"Hey, Jake!"

I turned around. It was Mickey.

"Where were you all morning?"

"I went to the hospital," I said as I kept walking.

"The hospital? Were you hurt or something?"

"No, not for me. I went to see about Luke."

"Why did you do that?" he demanded as he grabbed me by the shoulder and spun me around.

"I just wanted to see if he was okay," I said. I shook off his hand and started walking again. "I wanted to see if everybody was okay."

"He's gonna be fine, but he's going to miss some school," Mickey said.

"How do you know that?" I asked.

"They told us at the assembly."

"There was an assembly?"

"Yeah, first two periods of the morning."

That was probably good for me. Assemblies meant teachers weren't taking attendance and wouldn't have even known I wasn't there—at least for the first periods.

"And they mentioned Luke at the assembly?" I asked.

"Mentioned? That's what the whole assembly was about."

"You're joking…right?"

"Nope. The principal talked about the accident, and then the cop—"

"There was a cop?"

"Yeah. He did most of the talking and then they turned down the lights and he was showing pictures of car crashes on the screen. He said most of them were caused either by speeding or street racing. You should have seen some of those wrecks!"

"I've seen enough wrecks," I said. I had that one picture still seared in my memory and figured it would stay there for a long, long time.

"That's all everybody's been talking about all morning. I mentioned that Luke's car was really smashed up as bad as those ones in the slides and—"

"You said what?" I demanded as I stopped walking and spun around.

"I mentioned that we were there on the street and saw the accident."

"Why would you say that?"

"Don't worry, it isn't like I mentioned we were in the other—"

"Shut up!" I hissed.

Mickey looked around. "Nobody can hear me."

"Don't talk about it! Not now, not here, not at all. You've already been stupid!"

"And going to the hospital was bright?" Mickey asked.

"I just needed to know, that's all."

"If you'd been here this morning you would have known all that there was to know," he said.

"Did they talk about the woman being okay, that she had her baby and it's all right too?"

"No, they didn't mention that. That's great news."

"It is good—" I was cut off by the bell ringing. "Great. Just great. I'll see you sixth period."

I rushed off down the hall. My class was just up the stairs and to the right. I took the stairs two at a time, pushed open the door and raced down the corridor, skidding to a stop at the door to the class. Slowly, quietly, I opened it up and slipped in and—

"Good evening, Jake," Mr. Sloan said sarcastically. "Nice of you to finally join us."

"Sorry," I said as the door closed behind me.

"Do you have a late slip?" he asked.

"No…but I'm hardly late."

"You're a minute late. The difference between one o'clock and one minute after one."

"Come on, it's just one minute."

"One can mean a lot. Just like the difference between forty-nine and fifty is the difference between passing and failing," he said as he turned around and walked away. That was my mark last year—the mark that stopped me from passing math.

He was a terrible teacher and a rotten person. He was always saying nasty things to kids, including me.

"I guess that's not nearly as big as the difference between you and a good teacher!" I snapped.

"What did you say?" he demanded as he spun back around.

Instantly I regretted what I'd said, but what could I do now? He'd heard me. Everybody in the first five rows had heard me. Kids were giggling.

"What did you say?" he repeated.

"Nothing," I mumbled.

"If you said it, at least have the guts to repeat it to my face."

I took a deep breath. "It looks like you can't hear any better than you can teach."

"Get out!" he screamed. "Straight to the office! Now!"

I held my ground for another couple of seconds and glared at him. There was no point in arguing, so I turned around and left.

As I walked down the hall, I tried to figure out what was going to happen.

I hadn't done anything wrong all year, so they wouldn't suspend me. Or would they?

The office was full of kids waiting to get late slips or to sign in or out. There was no point in my standing in line because it wasn't like I was going back to class anyway. I'd just sit down and wait until the lineup was gone. I took a seat on the bench against the wall. What was the point in rushing?

"Jake, what are you doing here?"

I looked up. It was Miss Parsons, my guidance counselor. She was the last person I wanted to see. I was hoping she wouldn't even hear about this because I knew she'd be disappointed.

"Why aren't you in math?" she asked. "And don't look so surprised that I know you're supposed to be in math. I know everything!" She came out from behind the counter. "Just like I know that you weren't there for the assembly or the two morning classes after that," she said.

"I was at the hospital…seeing Luke."

"You did that? That is so nice."

Nice had nothing to do with it.

"I guess that's a good excuse for missing the morning. Why are you here now?"

"I was late for math," I said, looking down at the floor.

"Then why aren't you waiting in line for a late slip?" she asked.

"There's more," I admitted. "When he told me to go down to get a late slip, he said something."

"Probably something stupid," she muttered under her breath.

"What did you say?" I asked.

"Nothing that you were supposed to hear. So he said something, and then?"

"And then I said something back and he kicked me out."

She nodded her head. "That sounds like an old story. A story from last year. You haven't done that once this year. What's wrong?"

"Nothing's wrong."

"Yeah?" she asked. "You don't sound like nothing's wrong and you're not acting like nothing's wrong. Come with me," she said.

I trailed after her out of the main office, down the hall and into the guidance office. She led me into her little room and motioned for me to sit down as she took a seat behind her desk.

"Now, let's start again. Something is wrong. Something is bothering you…correct?"

Reluctantly, I nodded.

"Do you want to talk about it?" she asked.

"I would like to, but I can't."

"I see. And can you tell me why you can't?"

"I can't tell you that either," I said.

"I understand there are some things that aren't easy to discuss. I know it must be serious if it's troubling you this much."

"It is serious."

"Does it have to do with what happened to Luke?"

My eyes widened in shock. How did she know? What had she heard? Had she been talking to Mickey?

"Judging from your reaction, that was a lucky guess," she said.

"How did you know?" I asked.

"I just figured because you'd gone to the hospital, and you seem so upset now."

I didn't answer. I didn't know what to say.

"You don't have to say a word to me," she said. "I can tell that you're really troubled by something. It feels like you're trying to figure out what to do, trying to make some sort of decision."

Again I nodded ever so slightly.

"But it's okay that you don't discuss this problem with me, because you already know what to do."

"I do?"

"Yes." She stood up and walked around her desk, perching on the edge of it.

"Jake, I know you. I know you're a good person. That's why I went to bat for you last year. And because I know that, I know that whatever is bothering you, you will resolve it yourself."

"I will?" I asked in surprise.

"Of course you will. That is, if you know what's right. Do you know what the right thing to do is?" she asked.

I nodded. "I know."

"Is it a hard thing to do?"

Again I nodded.

"That makes it more difficult. That's where you learn about the character of a person. Anybody can do the right thing if it's easy or doesn't cost them anything."

I didn't even want to think about what could happen to me.

"Is there anything I can do to help?" she asked.

"I guess there is," I said. "Could I just be alone for a while, use your office, so I could think?"

"Certainly." She got up and went to the door. "While you're thinking, I'm going to see if I can straighten out the problem you had in math." She closed the door as she left.

I wished I could talk things over with her, but I knew I couldn't. I couldn't talk about this with anybody except Mickey, and that wasn't going to help me.

On one hand, everybody was going to be okay and absolutely nobody would ever know what had happened, what I'd done. Luke's mother had said such nice things about my going to the hospital, and Miss Parsons thought I was being so nice.

Eric Walters

Little did they know. And they wouldn't know…unless Luke regained his memory. Or Mickey blabbed to somebody.

I took a deep breath I knew what the right thing to do was. I knew it.

I took another deep breath and reached across Miss Parson's desk to pick up the phone. I dialed. It started to ring.

"Emergency Reponse," said a calm voice.

I didn't answer.

"This is Emergency Response," the voice came again.

"Hello," I said. "I'd like to talk to somebody. I'd like to talk to somebody about a car accident."

NEW
Orca Soundings novel

Blue Moon by Marilyn Halvorson

Bobbie Jo didn't set out to buy a limping blue roan mare—she wanted a colt she could train to barrel race. But the horse is a fighter, just like Bobbie Jo, and that's what made up her mind. Now all she has to do is train the sour old mare that obviously has a past. While she nurses the horse back to health and they get to know each other, Bobbie Jo realizes that the mare, now called Blue Moon, may have more history than she first thought. With the help of the enigmatic Cole McCall, she slowly turns the horse into a barrel racer. Then, when everything seems to be going well, she finds out the truth about Blue Moon and where she came from. Will Bobbie Jo be able to keep the horse? And will she find out why Cole seems to have so many secrets?

NEW
Orca Soundings novel

Thunderbowl by Lesley Choyce

Jeremy's band is hot—really hot. Thunderbowl is on the way up, and they have had their first big break. After beating archrivals The Mongrel Dogs in a battle of the bands, they have landed a long-term gig at a local bar, and now a record company might be interested. The only problem is that while Jeremy should be doing his homework and keeping up in school, he is spending most nights in a rowdy club, trying to keep the band together while his life is falling apart and he is pretending to be older than he actually is. Trying to balance his dreams of success with the hard realities of the music business, Jeremy is forced to make some hard choices as he works to make it in an adult world.

Zee's Way by **Kristin Butcher**

And that's when I realized there was someone standing near the end of the wall, watching me. I looked up. My mouth went dry. It was a man with a baseball bat.

Zee and his friends are angry, upset that they are not welcome at a new strip mall and that their old haunt has been replaced by stores that are off-limits to them and by storekeepers who treat them with distrust and disdain.

To get back at the merchants, and to let them know what he and his friends think, Zee paints graffiti on the wall of the hardware store. After the wall is repainted, Zee decides to repeat the vandalism, but this time with more artistic flair. When the store owner catches him in the act, he threatens to call the police—unless Zee agrees to repair the damage.

Orca Soundings

Death Wind by William Bell

Allie's life has just taken a turn for the worse. Not only do her parents fight all the time, but she is failing more classes than not and now she thinks she just might be pregnant. Unable to face up to her parents, she decides to run away. She hooks up with her old friend Razz, a professional skateboarder, and goes on the road. Razz is ranked number one, but constant confrontations with the challenger, Slammer, put Allie in some dangerous situations.

With the rivalry heating up, Razz and Allie head toward home—right into the path of a fierce tornado. To survive in the horror and destruction that follow the storm, Allie has to call on an inner strength she didn't know she had.

Orca Soundings

Sticks and Stones by Beth Goobie

No one expects Jujube to fight back when her reputation takes a beating.

Jujube is thrilled when Brent asks her out. She is not so happy when the rumors start flying at school. Pretty soon her name is showing up on bathroom walls, and everyone is snickering and sniping. When her mother gets involved, Jujube's reputation takes another hit. Deciding that someone has to take a stand, Jujube gathers all the other girls who are labeled sluts—and worse—and tries to impress on her fellow students the damage that can be done by assigning a label that reduces a person to an object.

Sticks and Stones is an inspiring—and enlightening—story about standing up for oneself and the importance of self-esteem and respect for others.

Other titles in the
ORCA SOUNDINGS series